Triceratops
try–SAIR–uh–tops

Velociraptor
veh–LOSS–ih–RAP–tor

Iguanodon
ig–WAN–oh–don

Peloroplites
PEL–or–OP–lih–teez

Corythosaurus
koh–RITH–uh–SAWR–us

Ankylosaurus
ang–KILE–uh–SAWR–us

Pachycephalosaurus
pak–ee–SEF–uh–loh–SAWR–us

Plateosaurus
PLAY–tee–uh–SAWR–us

Giganotosaurus
jig–ah–NOTE–ah–SAWR–us

To my wonderful wife

ACKNOWLEDGMENTS

Thank you to Dr. Luis Chiappe, Director of the Dinosaur Institute at the Natural History Museum
of Los Angeles County, for his expertise, attention to detail, and guidance.

Visit us on the Web! randomhousekids.com

Educators and librarians, for a variety of teaching tools, visit us at RHTeachersLibrarians.com

Library of Congress Cataloging-in-Publication Data
Names: Terranova, Michael-Paul, author.
Title: Roar : a dinosaur tour / Michael Paul.
Description: First Edition. | New York : Crown Books for Young Readers, [2018] | Audience: Ages 2–5. | Audience: Pre-school, excluding K.
Identifiers: LCCN 2017039185 | ISBN 978-1-5247-6698-6 (hc) | ISBN 978-1-5247-6700-6 (epub) | ISBN 978-1-5247-6699-3 (glb)
Subjects: LCSH: Dinosaurs—Juvenile literature.
Classification: LCC QE861.5 .T435 2018 | DDC 567.9—dc23

MANUFACTURED IN CHINA
10 9 8 7 6 5 4
First Edition

A NOTE ABOUT COLORS:
The latest research by paleontologists suggests that dinosaur species came in a multitude of colors, similar to modern birds. Although we can't know exactly what colors species were because intact skin, feathers, or scales have not been preserved, I was inspired by this research to show the dinosaurs in the book in a wild and wide range of colors.

ROAR

A Dinosaur Tour

Michael Paul

Crown Books for Young Readers
New York

Millions of years ago, dinosaurs walked the Earth.

KENTROSAURUS

There were many kinds of dinosaurs.

ALLOSAURUS

STYRACOSAURUS

LEAELLYNASAURA   STEGOSAURUS

COMPSOGNATHUS

There were little dinosaurs . . .

big dinosaurs . . .

TYRANNOSAURUS REX

and enormous dinosaurs.

SUPERSAURUS

Some dinosaurs walked on two legs . . .

while others walked on four legs.

TRICERATOPS

Some dinosaurs were fast . . .

VELOCIRAPTOR

IGUANODON

and other dinosaurs were slow.

Some kinds of dinosaurs lived alone . . .

PELOROPLITES

while others lived together in a family.

CORYTHOSAURUS

There were dinosaurs that used clubbed tails to protect themselves . . .

ANKYLOSAURUS

PACHYCEPHALOSAURUS

and others that used their heads.

Some dinosaurs shook the ground when they walked . . .

PLATEOSAURUS

while other dinosaurs shattered the silence with their loud roars!

GIGANOTOSAURUS

Today you can see their bones at the museum.

ANKYLOSAURUS

CARN

TAURUS

TRICERATOPS

Spiked Lizard

Strange Lizard

Spiked Lizard

Leaellyn's Lizard

Plated Lizard

Elegant Jaw

Tyrant Lizard King

Super Lizard

Meat-Eating Bull